STUDENT LEADE
STUDY GUIDE SERIES

LIFE

JAY STRACK

DAVID EDWARDS

NELSON IMPACT
A Division of Thomas Nelson Publishers
Since 1798

www.thomasnelson.com

Life: How to Get There from Here

Published by Nelson Impact, a Division of Thomas Nelson, Inc., P.O. Box 141000, Nashville, TN 37214.

ISBN 1-4185-0599-4

Printed in the United States of America

06 07 08 09 RRD 9 8 7 6 5 4 3 2 1

Page design by Crosslin Creative
2743 Douglas Lane, Thompsons Station, Tennessee 37179

CONTENTS

INTRODUCTION 5

KEY 6

1. MYTHS, LIES, AND FABRICATIONS ABOUT A PURE LIFE 9

2. PURITY FROM THE INSIDE OUT 23

3. BULLETPROOFING YOUR LIFE 39

4. SELF-DESTRUCTION 55

5. MENTAL FLOSS 69

6. THE PERSON YOU WANT TO BE WITH 83

7. IT MATTERS HOW YOU LIVE 97

8. IT'S NEVER WRONG TO DO RIGHT 111

NOTES 129

ABOUT THE AUTHORS 132

INTRODUCTION

"Get a life!"

How many times have you heard this phrase? It may be obnoxious, but actually, it's not such bad advice. Most people drift through life, lacking purpose and navigated only by the mantra of "whatever."

So what about you? Who or what is in control of your life? Our lives are heavily influenced by the choices we make. Often, when we do not make our own choices, the culture around us determines our choices for us. When we don't pray things through and plan our responses to certain situations, too often we allow other people or circumstances to determine whether or not we get what we want or dream about for our lives.

Dave Edwards and Jay Strack know what this struggle for control is like. Growing up, each author faced challenges, including learning difficulties, bad family situations, betrayals, faith issues, and abandonment. They've got some great lessons to share with you about living a life that is pure, joyful, and powerful.

The lessons in this study guide are designed to give you more than a clue about your destiny—they are specific road maps for fostering your passion and protecting your purity, all designed by a loving Creator who longs for the best for you.

So c'mon, take control of your life! Find out what God wants for you.

KEY

STUDENT LEADERSHIP UNIVERSITY CURRICULUM

Throughout this study guide, you will see several icons or headings that represent an idea, a statement, or a question that we want you to consider as you experience Scripture in this study guide series. Refer to the descriptions below to help you remember what the icons and headings mean.

transfuse (trans FYOOZ): to cause to pass from one to another; transmit

The goal of the lesson for the week.

Experience Scripture: Learning to really experience Scripture is the key element to "getting" who God is and all that He has in store for you.

infuse (in FYOOZ): to cause to be permeated with something (as a principle or quality) that alters usually for the better

Through journaling, group discussion, and personal study, experience Scripture as it permeates your heart and alters your life.

Future Tense Living: Your choices today will determine your future. Learn how to live with dynamic purpose and influence.

Attitude Reloaded: Rethink your attitude! Learn to replace self-centered, negative, or limited thoughts with positive, courageous, compassionate thoughts that are based on God's unlimited ability and power.

In His Steps: Every attitude and action of your life should begin with the questions, How would Jesus respond to this person and situation before me? What would He choose to do?

diffuse (di FYOOZ): to pour out and permit or cause to spread freely; to extend, scatter

Once God's Word is infused into your heart, it will pour forth to others without restraint. In this section, explore what that looks like in your daily life.

Called to Lead: Learn how to lead others as Christ would.

Called to Stand: Know what you believe and learn how to defend it with clarity and strength.

Called to Share: Sharing truth and serving others are results of a transformed life. How can you share with others the awesome things you're learning?

One Thing: Consider ONE THING you can do this week to make a difference in your life and/or the life of another.

Power up for the week with this focused truth.

CHAPTER 1

MYTHS, LIES, AND FABRICATIONS ABOUT A PURE LIFE

KEY SCRIPTURE

Let no one despise your youth, but be an example to the believers in word, in conduct, in love, in spirit, in faith, in purity.

—1 Timothy 4:12

COULD THIS BE YOU?

James J. Braddock was nicknamed "Cinderella Man" by a reporter during his 1935 comeback.[1] In his first round as a professional boxer, Braddock emerged a winner. But in time, he started losing the majority of his fights. When the Great Depression hit in 1929, unable to make money as a boxer, Braddock left the ring and returned to the docks so he could provide for his family.

> If a man's mind becomes pure, his surroundings will also become pure.
> —Ancient proverb

The rough years of the Depression affected the entire country. Many people were starving, men were being laid off daily, and families were sending their children to the homes of relatives in the hopes they might have a better chance of surviving. When Braddock was unable to find work, the proud ex-boxer swallowed his pride and applied for relief. He was ashamed to be on welfare, but his wife and three children needed food.

Finally, in 1934, Braddock got a break. He stepped in as a replacement boxer and won the fight by knocking out his opponent. His success as a heavyweight boxer continued from 1937 into 1938.[2] During the time he was on assistance, Braddock kept a running tally of all the money he'd been given. Now that he was able to provide for his family as a boxer, he went back to the welfare office and returned the money he'd been given.[3] Braddock's thoughts were, "They paid me. I returned it; let them give it to somebody else because they were good enough to give it to me. [I was in] a spot where I could pay it back."[4]

God doesn't remove the consequences of sin, but He does walk through them with you.

WHY KNOW IT?

- Only 6 percent of all teens believe that there are moral absolutes.[5]
- Only 9 percent of self-described born-again teens believe that moral truth is absolute.[6]

transfuse (trans FYOOZ): to cause to pass from one to another; transmit

There has been so much emphasis put on sexual purity that we may forget how we actually get there. It begins with a pure heart.

The Christian does choose a different lifestyle than the culture—a meaningful lifestyle. We have to know why we believe and stand for purity, or ultimately we get lost in the crowd culture.

Purity is no different than any other goal. It has to be thought through and broken down into manageable steps. In setting any goal, there are four questions to ask:

1. What do I want to do?
2. Why do I want to do it?
3. When will I get it done?
4. How will I accomplish it?

If you take a group of people and allow them to vote on which of those four are the most important, you will get four different answers. *What* seems like the logical choice—you have to know exactly, specifically what you want to accomplish and then the others will naturally follow, right? *How* seems logical—you have to know how to accomplish the goal. But logic and reason do not drive us to the finish line. It is only when we have a unmistakable definition of *why* we want to begin a project, try a hobby, make a friend, or learn something new that we are able to not only begin it, but also to finish it. *Why* drives the *what* and *how* of every goal.

GROUP DISCUSSION

Define *why* purity is important to you. Write two to three sentences about it here:

Now that you have a strong *why* on paper, dwell on it often, think it, tell it, and focus on it.

Those efforts will give you ownership of this important quality so that it's not your mom's idea or the church's idea, but your heart's call.

Casting down arguments and every high thing that exalts itself against the knowledge of God, bringing every thought into captivity to the obedience of Christ. **—2 Corinthians 10:5**

Popular myths about purity have to be destroyed in your personal life. Quit arguing with yourself, and stop allowing evil reasoning to rob you of a powerful life. This reasoning takes us right to the edge of our convictions—how far can we go and not get caught? How far is too far? If you play on the edge, you will one day fall off the edge. Once and for all, accept the whole truth and nothing but the truth.

infuse (in FYOOZ): to cause to be permeated with something (as a principle or quality) that alters usually for the better

The mind is a powerful motivator. It has the power to encourage or discourage. It is where the journey to a devoted heart begins. When the mind is overcome and taken captive, it lays down all authority of its own and walks in obedience to Christ. Filling the mind with positive *why* is essential, but so is destroying the lies that stand in our way as obstacles to the goal of a pure life.

MYTHS, LIES, AND FABRICATIONS ABOUT A PURE LIFE

Myth 1: Purity is only about what I do sexually.

Let no one despise your youth, but be an example to the believers in word, in conduct, in love, in spirit, in faith, in purity. **—1 Timothy 4:12**

Truth: Purity is about example.

Paul speaks to young Timothy, who is probably close to your age, and says, "Just because you are young doesn't mean you can't be an example to others."

- ✦ To be an example is to be a pattern for others to follow.
- ✦ It is a huge responsibility, one that only a pure heart can fulfill.

Truth: Purity is about the influence you can have on others.

Paul tells Timothy to be a positive influence for purity in both his speech and in his actions.

Did you know that *sex* is the most frequently searched word on the Internet?

When influencing others for good is an essential daily goal, then we will be inspired to live a life of purity.

ASK YOURSELF

Ask yourself, "Why do I want to live a pure life?" You have to have clear, sure answers before you can be successful in this area. "Because I'm supposed to" will leave you powerless. Choose to live far above the culture standards because it is important to you to do so.

Truth: Purity is about what or who you love.

- ✦ Who or what holds your affections?
- ✦ What type of lifestyle are you drawn to, do you think about, and do you "love"?
- ✦ The authentic mark of a Christian is a pure love for people, without regard for selfish gain or love in return.

Truth: Purity is about attitude.

Attitude may be the one thing holding you back from living a pure life. If you allow bitterness, anger, jealousy, or other negative emotions or thoughts to rule, you cannot have a pure heart.

What ONE THING (attitude or negative emotion) in your life might be keeping you from a pure heart?

Myth 2: It's too late for me. I've made too many mistakes.

> *"Come now, and let us reason together," says the* Lord*, "Though your sins are like scarlet, they shall be as white as snow; though they are red like crimson, they shall be as wool."* **—Isaiah 1:18**

Truth: This argument is not only a lie, but it calls God a liar.

To say, "It's too late" is to speak of Christ's death on the cross as though it didn't happen. He came from heaven to earth, suffered shame, humiliation, pain, and rose from the dead, all for one reason—that you could be forgiven! This lie discounts the forgiveness of God down to nothing.

Truth: You cannot measure the forgiveness and grace of God by your own ability to forgive.

The Lord tells us, "Sit down and let's talk about this." He offers to remove the stain on your life that's been marked with a permanent red dye and make it white like snow. His is a complete, restoring forgiveness.

How does your attitude toward purity influence the way you forgive others?

diffuse (di FYOOZ): to pour out and permit or cause to spread freely; to extend, scatter

Myth 3: If I choose to do the purity thing, everything will be "all good" all at once.

Do not be deceived, God is not mocked;
for whatever a man sows, that he
will also reap. **—Galatians 6:7**

Truth: The depth of God's mercy and forgiveness does not give us permission to keep sinning.

God is "not mocked," Galatians 6:7 says. In other words, He will not allow His holiness to become an option.

Truth: The pure heart accepts responsibility for previous choices and the resulting consequences.

A person with a pure heart is willing to make whatever amends necessary with people. For example, you may decide to become morally pure once and for all, but...

- ✦ The people you hurt must be asked for forgiveness.
- ✦ The person you showed the wrong example to must be talked to.
- ✦ The results of your sexual immorality (STDs, pregnancy, guilt and shame, sinning against a person) will have to be dealt with.

The good news is that Christ will walk through each of those situations with you because His grace is more than sufficient to help you do the right thing and restore your testimony.

Myth 4: God will give me whatever I want, if I just stay pure.

For I desire mercy and not sacrifice,
and the knowledge of God more than
burnt offerings. **—Hosea 6:6**

Truth: God doesn't owe you anything.

Live for Him because you love Him, because it's the best choice. Otherwise, forget it.

Myth 5: Purity is about the things I don't do.

For the Lord does not see as man sees, for
man looks at the outward appearance, but the
Lord looks at the heart. **—1 Samuel 16:7**

Truth: Purity is about the private world, not just what you don't do outwardly.

The Bible tells us, "The Lord looks on the heart." You might lie to yourself and tell yourself what a great person you are, but God knows the innermost thoughts and intents of the heart.

Which purity myth holds a position of power in your life?

Why do you think you have chosen to believe it?

Purity is about an undying loyalty to Christ and His will. Think of the soldier fighting for his country even when he is wounded and tired and his belly is empty. His loyalty defies circumstances.

Now that you understand the truth about purity, be ready to share the forgiveness of God with those who may be facing the consequences of their choices. Explain that God's grace will walk with them through the consequences and that you will be their friend.

Purity is not just about the body; it's about the whole person, beginning in the private world.

PRIVATE WORLD DEVOTIONS

MONDAY: See it. Read the surrounding passages or chapter for the Key Scripture so that you can get an understanding of the background and context. This helps you to really ***see*** the verse.

TUESDAY: Hear it. Read the daily Key Scripture and/or surrounding passage out loud, putting your name in, if applicable. For example, John *can do all things through Christ. Thieves have come to destroy* John, *but Jesus has come that* John *might have eternal life.*

WEDNESDAY: Write it. Write the verse and then what it says about:

- ***Others:*** Respond, serve, and love as Jesus would.
- ***Me:*** Specific attitudes, choices, or habits.
- ***God:*** His love, mercy, holiness, peace, joy, etc.

PRIVATE WORLD JOURNAL

I am grateful for—I praise you for—I am feeling—I am thinking—I need help with

PRIVATE WORLD DEVOTIONS *(Continued)*

THURSDAY: Memorize it. Take the verse with you—write it on a card or put it in your phone, iPod, or PDA. Go over it throughout the day so that it begins to *live* in your heart and mind.

FRIDAY: Pray it. Personalize the verse as you pray for yourself or for others or in praise to God. To pray is literally "to think about." Try thinking out loud or writing in your **PRIVATE WORLD JOURNAL.**

SATURDAY: Share it. Ask the Lord to bring someone to mind or in your path today who needs good news. Don't be shy—just let it out! Whether you IM, write, text, tell, or send it, the joy of God's Word will flow from your heart into theirs.

PRAYER REQUESTS

Date	Name	Need	Answer

PRIVATE WORLD JOURNAL

I am grateful for—I praise you for—I am feeling—I am thinking—I need help with

NOTES

CHAPTER 2

PURITY FROM THE INSIDE OUT

KEY SCRIPTURE

I will sing of mercy and justice; To You, O LORD, I will sing praises. I will behave wisely in a perfect way. Oh, when will you come to me? I will walk within my house with a perfect heart. I will set nothing wicked before my eyes; I hate the work of those who fall away; It shall not cling to me.

—Psalm 101:1–3

COULD THIS BE YOU?

Lance Shelby, a high school senior from Minnesota, was on his way to work when he saw the accident. It was raining heavily, and the car in front of him hydroplaned out of control, went off the road, and plunged into a lake. Shelby's first instinct was to pull over, dive in to the lake, and swim immediately to the car. The driver had already escaped and was helping his wife out of the window as she cried, "I can't swim!" Lance assured her, "Hold on and it will be fine," as he swam with her, using the other arm, to shallow water where they could stand.

> If we take care in the beginning, the end will take care of itself.
>
> —Ken Blanchard

When interviewed afterward about the situation, Lance said that when he saw the accident, he figured it wouldn't matter if he was late for work. "I didn't know it was deep. I just swam out there. I felt that God used me to help those people. You never know when God is going to use you in a situation."[1]

In a moment of decision, Lance made the right choice. What was already in his heart came out when he was emotionally squeezed, and he responded with a pure heart, despite the danger to himself.

WHY KNOW IT?

- 50 percent of Americans believe that anyone who is "generally good or does enough good things for others during their life, will earn a place in heaven."[2]

transfuse (trans FYOOZ): to cause to pass from one to another; transmit

When you squeeze a tube of toothpaste, toothpaste comes out because that's what's inside. Similarly, when a person is squeezed through stress or temptation, what comes out is what's inside. The private world of a person is revealed in trials based on their actions, responses, or reactions to the situation. Students are no different.

If we expect to make good choices, represent Christ well, and remain morally pure, then we have to put some effort into getting there and staying there.

- Every moment makes a contribution to who you are and who you are becoming.
- To have a life under control, you must have the moments of life under control.

It sounds like hard work, and it is. But the reward fuels you into more resolve about choosing who you are rather than being a victim of the past or making stupid mistakes. It's like the auto preventive maintenance slogan: "You can pay me now, or you can pay me later."

I will sing of mercy and justice; to You, O LORD, I will sing praises. I will behave wisely in a perfect way. Oh, when will You come to me? I will walk within my house with a perfect heart. I will set nothing wicked before my eyes; I hate the work of those who fall away; it shall not cling to me. A perverse heart shall depart from me; I will not know wickedness. Whoever secretly slanders his neighbor, him I will destroy; the one who has a haughty look and a proud heart, him I will not endure. My eyes shall be on the faithful of the land, that they may dwell with me; he who walks in a perfect way, he shall serve me. He who works deceit shall not dwell within my house; he who tells lies shall not continue in my presence. Early I will destroy all the wicked of the land, that I may cut off all the evildoers from the city of the LORD. **—Psalm 101**

Once we understand who God is—His holiness, mercy, justice, forgiveness, and goodness—we find a pure, energizing motive to live holy.

infuse (in FYOOZ): to cause to be permeated with something (as a principle or quality) that alters usually for the better

Purity Is a Choice

Nine times in Psalm 101, David says, "I will." Two very small words—but one very big, powerful decision. "I will" involves the heart, mind, body, and spirit.

I will . . .

- ✦ If no one else does, I will.
- ✦ If no one else comes with me, I will.
- ✦ If the odds are against me, I will.
- ✦ I have made the choice.

In Psalm 34:1, David wrote, "I will bless the Lord at all times; his praise shall continually be in my mouth." This declaration may be the key to living a successful, larger-than-life adventure for God.

Decide now—
up or down,
good or bad,
alone or in a crowd—
I will give praise to God.

In the midst of constant noise and distraction—"Hey, buy this! Try that! Look at this!"—you can develop the intentional habit of praise as you consider God's personal intervention in your life.

How much time do you spend listening to secular music every day? Decide today to do ONE THING different this week:

- ✦ Replace one secular song with a praise song, and sing it twice as personal praise.
- ✦ Eliminate one secular song and read a psalm instead.

In Psalm 101, David wrote of a deep, passionate relationship with God. How do you get one of those? It is the result of living the Christian life.

Purity Begins with Praise

I will sing of mercy and justice. **—Psalm 101:1**

David sang with gratitude about:

- ✦ the mercy of God—His unconditional forgiveness;
- ✦ the justice of God—that God loves him enough to correct him.

> **When you praise God, you redirect your thinking from evil and negative to pure and positive.**

This was not a song he found in a book or heard with his youth group. It came from a reflective heart.

Don't forget to journal your thoughts. Journaling is a great way to self-discovery. You can look and see who you are right now and who you want to become as your heart comes to life in black and white (or lots of colors, if you choose).

Taking the time to do this can make the difference between:

- ✦ "hanging on" in your moral life, or
- ✦ walking in confidence and strength in moral choices.

Don't take shortcuts when all around you is bombardment against holiness.

Journal one sentence here:

- ✦ about your faith:

✦ about your thoughts of God:

✦ about friends:

✦ about your church:

Purity Focuses on Who God Is

To You, O LORD, I will sing praises. **—Psalm 101:1**

To have a pure heart and life, focus on God:

✦ *His character*. To be *holy* is to be like God—to have a personality, will, and character like God.

What is set before the eyes can easily make its way to the heart, so protect yourself.

✦ *His gift of eternal life*. Jesus Christ died for you, rose from the dead, and gives you the gift of salvation.

✦ *His unconditional love*. God loves you as His child, and nothing can separate you.

✦ His personal intervention in your life.

Focusing on the character of God results in awe and gratitude, and this brings about a desire to actively seek purity.

GROUP DISCUSSION

If God's holiness is the standard, what does it say about sexual experimentation and the "how-far-is-too-far" argument?

Purity Transforms the Private World

I will walk within my house with a perfect heart. I will set nothing wicked before my eyes. **—Psalm 101:2–3**

Ironically, David's eyes are exactly what got him into trouble. At home, walking about on a warm evening, he *saw* Bathsheba taking a bath on a roof. He could have turned away. He could have walked back inside, but he chose to keep looking, and a disastrous choice overtook him.

When David lost the battle for purity,

- ✦ His choice led to adultery, murder, betrayal, and hypocrisy;
- ✦ David's walk with God was never quite the same;
- ✦ His children did not choose to serve the Lord.

Create in me a clean heart, O God, and renew a steadfast spirit within me.
—Psalm 51:10

How do my pure decisions and actions help to influence the decisions and actions of my friends?

How am I protecting my friends by committing to maintain a pure life?

Write below the name of one person you know who could be encouraged to live a pure life if your example was more consistent.

Pray:

- ✦ For your own consistency
- ✦ For their victory in the heart

diffuse (di FYOOZ): to pour out and permit or cause to spread freely; to extend, scatter

Purity Requires Separation

I hate the work of those who fall away;
it shall not cling to me. A perverse heart
shall depart from me; I will not know
wickedness. **—Psalm 101:3–4**

In pretty strong language, David says, “I hate the actions of those who walk away from God.”

- ✦ Notice that he doesn’t say he hates the person, but he does hate the action.
- ✦ The person who seeks purity is not drawn to evil. He or she is repelled by it.

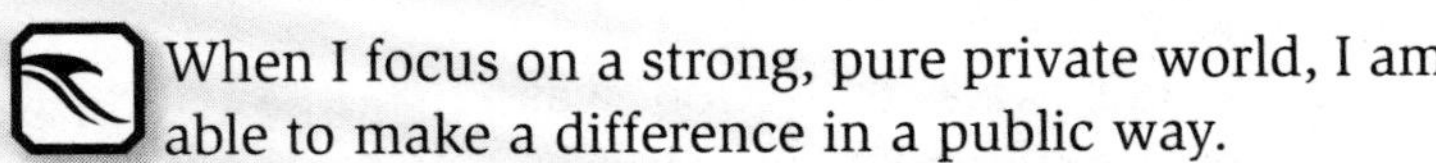

When I focus on a strong, pure private world, I am able to make a difference in a public way.

What are some of the choices I can make in a public way?

- ✦ At school:
- ✦ At home:
- ✦ At church:

How do these choices affect my reputation as a leader?

ASK YOURSELF

If you are lacking purity power in your thought life or daily choices, then ask yourself, "What do I love? What do I like to think about? What do I get excited about doing?"

> Purity of the soul cannot be lost without consent.
> —St. Augustine

✦ When you love the pure characteristics of God, think about the holiness of God, and desire to serve others, then, like David, what you hate stands so far out that it's easy to walk away from it.

Purity Loves Pure Company

He who walks in a perfect way, he shall serve me. He who works deceit shall not dwell within my house; he who tells lies shall not continue in my presence. **—Psalm 101:6–7**

David insists that he will not hang out with those who do not seek purity.

- ✦ He doesn't want them in the house.
- ✦ He won't choose them as friends.
- ✦ He will not hire them.

But where do you find pure people? *The church* is an absolute necessity for the pure-in-heart Christian.

- ✦ Group praise and worship is a strengthening experience. You can deepen your connection with God and other believers when the Holy Spirit joins in with the spirit of the group.
- ✦ Group Bible study can help you build spiritual bonds with each other and strengthen your relationship with God.
- ✦ Pure friendships bring out the best in you and want the best for you. Think of your closest friends—those who call, IM, hang out with, and check up on you. If your closest friends share your commitment to a pure heart and life, they will stand beside you in good and bad times.

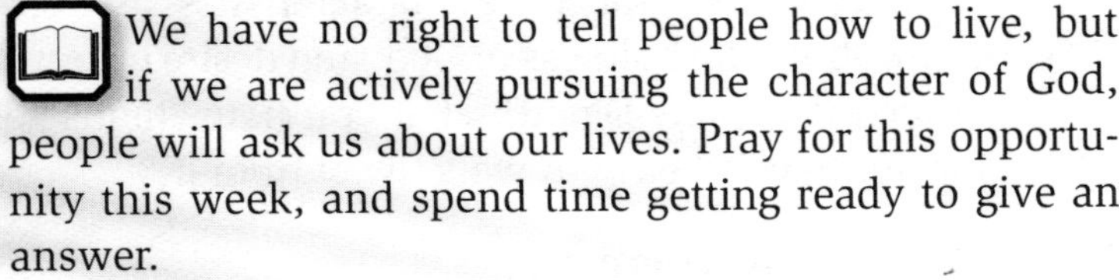

We have no right to tell people how to live, but if we are actively pursuing the character of God, people will ask us about our lives. Pray for this opportunity this week, and spend time getting ready to give an answer.

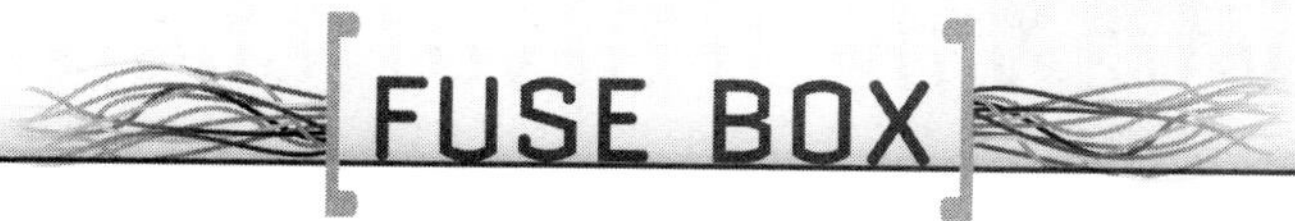

Purity is expressing my love for God in every area of my life.

PRIVATE WORLD DEVOTIONS

MONDAY: See it. Read the surrounding passages or chapter for the Key Scripture so that you can get an understanding of the background and context. This helps you to really ***see*** the verse.

TUESDAY: Hear it. Read the daily Key Scripture and/or surrounding passage out loud, putting your name in, if applicable. For example, <u>John</u> *can do all things through Christ. Thieves have come to destroy* <u>John</u>, *but Jesus has come that* <u>John</u> *might have eternal life.*

WEDNESDAY: Write it. Write the verse and then what it says about:

- ***Others:*** Respond, serve, and love as Jesus would.
- ***Me:*** Specific attitudes, choices, or habits.
- ***God:*** His love, mercy, holiness, peace, joy, etc.

PRIVATE WORLD JOURNAL

I am grateful for—I praise you for—I am feeling—I am thinking—I need help with

PRIVATE WORLD DEVOTIONS *(Continued)*

THURSDAY: Memorize it. Take the verse with you—write it on a card or put it in your phone, iPod, or PDA. Go over it throughout the day so that it begins to *live* in your heart and mind.

FRIDAY: Pray it. Personalize the verse as you pray for yourself or for others or in praise to God. To pray is literally "to think about." Try thinking out loud or writing in your **PRIVATE WORLD JOURNAL.**

SATURDAY: Share it. Ask the Lord to bring someone to mind or in your path today who needs good news. Don't be shy—just let it out! Whether you IM, write, text, tell, or send it, the joy of God's Word will flow from your heart into theirs.

PRAYER REQUESTS

Date	Name	Need	Answer

PRIVATE WORLD JOURNAL

I am grateful for—I praise you for—I am feeling—I am thinking—I need help with

NOTES

BULLETPROOFING YOUR LIFE

KEY SCRIPTURE

No temptation has overtaken you except such as is common to man; but God is faithful, who will not allow you to be tempted beyond what you are able, but with the temptation will also make the way of escape, that you may be able to bear it.

—1 Corinthians 10:13

COULD THIS BE YOU?

At a Subway restaurant in San Diego, bulletproof glass separated the customers from the employees. And since there was no speaker, there were misunderstandings. For example:

JOE: I'll have a ham and cheese.

SANDWICH ARTIST: Don't worry, you can sneeze.

JOE: No, I said a ham and cheese.

SANDWICH ARTIST: So what do you want to eat today?

JOE: A ham and cheese!

SANDWICH ARTIST: Oh. Do you want cheese on that?

JOE: Yes!

SANDWICH ARTIST: What?

JOE: Yes!

SANDWICH ARTIST: I still can't hear. What do you want?

JOE: Ham and cheese!

SANDWICH ARTIST: Hold the cheese?

JOE: Look, I'll just have a Coke.

SANDWICH ARTIST: Do you want cheese on that?[1]

Can you bulletproof your *life* and still have friends, be a normal student, and enjoy life? Yes, you can—and you must.

WHY KNOW IT?

- One-sixth of today's teens (17 percent) said their church experience had imparted core religious beliefs from the Bible.[2]
- 75 percent of prime time television in the 1999–2000 season included sexual content.[3]

transfuse (trans FYOOZ): to cause to pass from one to another; transmit

In an effort to protect hackers from breaking into computer networks, new software has been developed called BulletProof©. It promises total control over where files go, activity and traffic monitoring, and user space limitations on certain areas of a computer.

Our computerlike minds need the same kind of protection, and the good news is that it is readily available. This type of protection comes in the form of the Word of God, and it can definitely be downloaded for free.

We know about the power of this Word, but many of us have not installed it in our heart and mind, opened the files, and allowed it to do its work. This powerful

Word of God will take control of what is filed in your mind, monitor your activities, and limit the amount of space your heart can dedicate to a specific area.

Then Jesus went into the temple of God and drove out all those who bought and sold in the temple, and overturned the tables of the money changers and the seats of those who sold doves. And He said to them, "It is written, 'My house shall be called a house of prayer,' but you have made it a 'den of thieves.'" Then the blind and the lame came to Him in the temple, and He healed them. **—Mathew 21:12–13**

One of the greatest challenges we face in allowing God's Word to work in our lives is that we must first delete our personal agenda to allow God to have His complete way in us.

infuse (in FYOOZ): to cause to be permeated with something (as a principle or quality) that alters usually for the better

To bulletproof your life, you must first *protect your heart.*

Pure Motives

Jesus drove the people out of the temple because they had the wrong motive for being there. He saw their agenda, and He could not allow it to continue.

Notice that both the buyers and the sellers were driven out by Jesus. Both had come pretending to be there for spiritual purposes. In this case, it was to offer a sacrifice in obedience to the command God had given Moses. The buying and selling of doves in the temple made the obligation more convenient to fulfill. Buyers could just bring in a few coins rather than go to the trouble and expense of bringing their own animal.

- ✦ For the buyers, it fulfilled a religious obligation.
- ✦ For the sellers, it was a way to make money and mask themselves as religious people.

Why do I come to church? What is my true motive for being here?

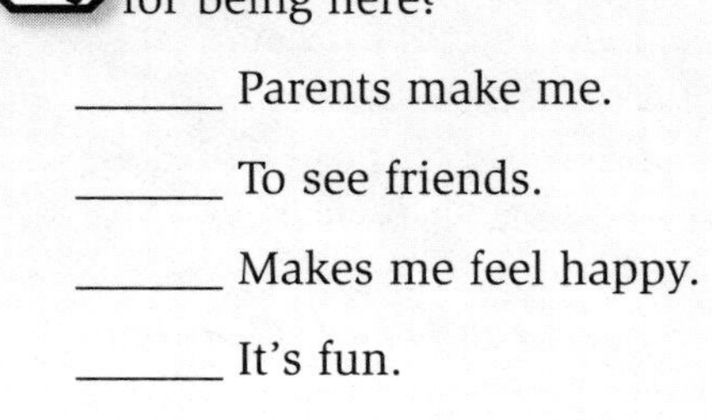

______ Parents make me.

______ To see friends.

______ Makes me feel happy.

______ It's fun.

______ Other:

Genuine Worship

Buying the sacrifice in the temple might not seem like a big deal to you, but it was to Jesus. It was *a spiritual counterfeit.*

The house of prayer had become a social club, a place to bargain, and not a place to worship. Walking into the temple, handing over some coins, and dropping off the sacrifice fulfilled the literal act of obedience, but not the spiritual one.

Sacrifice is the giving of self, not the fulfillment of an obligation.

Christ wants you to understand that true confession of sin and genuine worship produces pure hearts. Jesus confronts sin to make us clean, not comfortable, because He has a better plan for our lives.

Many students are like those temple dwellers Christ encountered. They come to church, drop off an offering, hug a few people, and maybe even open their Bibles, but they don't intend to be changed or participate in true worship.

Christ is after something greater in our lives:

We Want ...	**He Wants ...**
Our prayers answered	Our character changed
To feel good	To make us well
To express our individuality	To conform us to His image
God to speak to us about our future	To give us power in the present

What insecurities are you holding on to (failure, rejection, shame, etc.)?

> Motivation gets you going and habit gets you there. Make motivation a habit, and you will get there more quickly and have more fun on the trip.
>
> —Zig Ziglar

What feelings cause you to lower your guard to temptation (loneliness, anger, insecurity, etc.)?

Notice that as soon as the temple was cleansed, it was able to be used for God's purpose. It became the place where people found healing by faith in Christ.

The temple of Christ today is your heart. It is where He lives. It is where worship takes place. He wants to establish purity in the temple of your heart because:

✦ He wants the Father to be honored.

✦ He has something greater for you.

diffuse (di FYOOZ): to pour out and permit or cause to spread freely; to extend, scatter

To bulletproof your life, you must *identify where the shots are coming from.*

Past Failures
The more detail you allow yourself to see of a past failure, the clearer vision you have of a successful future against temptation. Failure can be a powerful teacher if you let it be.

No one likes to talk about failure. In fact, we prefer to pretend like it didn't happen. But what if we examine the failure and ask, "What can I learn from this?" We don't have to talk to others about it, but if we look at it head-on, we just might learn to be successful the next time.

Present Struggles

What temptations are you struggling with right now?

____

____

____

When I fight temptation, I cannot take the opinion of the crowd into account. I must base my life on God's perfect will, as already shown in the Scriptures.

GROUP DISCUSSION

To understand what's going on, ask:

- *Why* am I tempted?
- *What* was I thinking when it happened?
- *Where* was I?
- *Who* was I with?
- *How* did I feel?

You can ignore temptation until it topples you, or you can face temptation and win. Ignoring it is easier, but the consequences are much harder to deal with. Facing it is more difficult, but there are no consequences! You choose.

Being in the Wrong Place at the Wrong Time
Temptation comes and goes, teases and entices, but there is good news: *God is faithful!* The enemy will launch every possible attack and use every imaginable weapon to try to defeat you, but God is greater and wiser than Satan.

USE SAFETY EQUIPMENT AND KNOW AVAILABLE ESCAPE ROUTES

Safety Equipment:

Guarded Heart—Stay on alert by choosing beforehand what you will do in a situation.

Understand what the will of God is—Pure heart, pure mind, pure motives.

Accountability partners and friends—Trusted friends provide strong protection.

Read the Word—Fill your mind and heart with absolute truth.

Depend on the Holy Spirit—He will convict you of impending sin. Just listen.

ASK YOURSELF

Which of these are you doing without?

What ONE THING do you need to change?

When will you make this change?

How will you do it?

______

______

______

Who will you do it with?

______

______

______

Escape Routes:

Say "no!" Decide beforehand what you will and will not do, and where you will and will not go.

Plan your time. Work on your dreams; make new friends. Deliberately choose what you will do with your free time.

Ask for help from good friends. If temptation gets too strong, call a friend who will help to lead you away.

List three people you can call for help when you are tempted:

1. ______
2. ______
3. ______

How can you prevent bulletproofing from isolating you from the world you are trying to reach for Christ?

_________ Show concern for others.

_________ Be a good listener.

_________ Be consistent in your example.

_________ Talk often of God's personal, unconditional love for others.

_________ All of the above!

[FUSE BOX]

Unstructured time spent with an unguarded heart is the same as playing spiritual Russian roulette.

Right place = the temple

NOTES

Wrong sacrifice = money instead of self

PRIVATE WORLD DEVOTIONS

MONDAY: See it. Read the surrounding passages or chapter for the Key Scripture so that you can get an understanding of the background and context. This helps you to really ***see*** the verse.

TUESDAY: Hear it. Read the daily Key Scripture and/or surrounding passage out loud, putting your name in, if applicable. For example, John *can do all things through Christ. Thieves have come to destroy* John, *but Jesus has come that* John *might have eternal life.*

WEDNESDAY: Write it. Write the verse and then what it says about:

- ✦ ***Others:*** Respond, serve, and love as Jesus would.
- ✦ ***Me:*** Specific attitudes, choices, or habits.
- ✦ ***God:*** His love, mercy, holiness, peace, joy, etc.

PRIVATE WORLD JOURNAL

I am grateful for—I praise you for—I am feeling—I am thinking—I need help with

PRIVATE WORLD DEVOTIONS *(Continued)*

THURSDAY: Memorize it. Take the verse with you—write it on a card or put it in your phone, iPod, or PDA. Go over it throughout the day so that it begins to *live* in your heart and mind.

FRIDAY: Pray it. Personalize the verse as you pray for yourself or for others or in praise to God. To pray is literally "to think about." Try thinking out loud or writing in your **PRIVATE WORLD JOURNAL.**

SATURDAY: Share it. Ask the Lord to bring someone to mind or in your path today who needs good news. Don't be shy—just let it out! Whether you IM, write, text, tell, or send it, the joy of God's Word will flow from your heart into theirs.

PRAYER REQUESTS

Date	Name	Need	Answer

PRIVATE WORLD JOURNAL

I am grateful for—I praise you for—I am feeling—I am thinking—I need help with

NOTES

CHAPTER 4

SELF-DESTRUCTION

KEY SCRIPTURE

Casting down arguments and every high thing that exalts itself against the knowledge of God, bringing every thought into captivity to the obedience of Christ.

—2 Corinthians 10:5

COULD THIS BE YOU?

Brad was a high school virgin, and he planned to stay that way. One day, he was bored and decided to go dumpster diving on the local military base where his father was stationed. Usually he found cool stuff to trade or sell on eBay, but today he found something different. One box contained at least ten pornographic magazines, something Brad had never seen.

His first thought was to walk away, but the cover captions and photos drew him in completely. He was mesmerized by what he saw, and he couldn't wait to look again. Brad carefully hid the magazines behind a loose board in a nearby building. No one would know. It was just curiosity.

Every weekend, Brad would sneak away to his stash of porn. He knew it was getting out of hand, but he couldn't stop. He no longer saw women as friends—they were objects to be fantasized over and used for self-gratification. Everything about Brad's moods changed: he was angry with his family, couldn't keep a friendship, and had frequent bouts of depression. He hated the double life he was living.

Reflecting on the experience later, Brad said, "If I could do it over again, I would never have looked."

WHY KNOW IT?

- ✦ The average American adolescent will view nearly 14,000 sexual references per year.[1]

transfuse (trans FYOOZ): to cause to pass from one to another; transmit

Self-destruction is most dangerous when it affects the areas of our values, successes, and confidence. Most Christians are on the defense against the outside forces that try to entrap our minds, but we are not so good at the inner voices that break down truth with distorted language. We rarely just walk out and choose the worst; instead, we convince ourselves that it's "not so bad" and give in. Our good intentions are overthrown.

King Solomon loved many foreign women, as well as the daughter of Pharaoh: women of the Moabites, Ammonites, Edomites, Sidonians, and Hittites—from the nations of whom the LORD had said to the children of Israel, "You shall not intermarry with them, nor they with you. Surely they will turn away your hearts after their gods." **—1 Kings 11:1–2**

infuse (in FYOOZ): to cause to be permeated with something (as a principle or quality) that alters usually for the better

"It Won't Happen to Me"

Solomon allowed foreign women to bring their beliefs into his home, but he never intended to change his ways of worship. He thought his wives' pagan gods could sit in the background of his life. But Solomon was deceived by his own perceived ability to control himself and the influences he allowed into his home and his country. By overestimating his ability to control the influence, he fell prey to the "It won't happen to me" syndrome.

- ✦ We think that we can allow a small compromise in a strong area of our lives.
- ✦ To justify our actions, we tell ourselves that it can easily be stopped if it does become a problem.
- ✦ These compromises open the door to rebellion against God's principles for our lives.
- ✦ At first, we naively think we can turn around; but only after we are in too far do we see the path to willing self-destruction. And then, it's usually too late.

 There are guaranteed consequences to rebellion:

- ✦ God will deal with you.
- ✦ It will catch up with you.
- ✦ Your life will become counterproductive.

"I Know What God Says, but I Don't Care"

We make choices for ourselves; no one makes them for us. When we willfully turn away from what God has told us, we have made a personal decision to ignore God. We think we can do whatever we want and that God just can't understand how we feel. *He's too heavenly minded,* we think.

In 1 Kings 11, God had already warned the Israelites about the dangers of bringing foreign gods into the home: "... The Lord had said to the children of Israel, 'You shall not intermarry with them, nor they with you. Surely they will turn away your hearts after their gods.'"

Solomon thought, *God just doesn't get it. I need these women.* When he made the choice to bring foreign gods into his life, Solomon gave in to the vicious voices.

- ✦ **Lust**. Solomon loved these women, but it was not a pure love. His actions were encouraged by his lust. The Israelite women at home dressed modestly and believed in moral purity. But the foreign women were loose in morals, speech, and dress. In an effort to control his lust, Solomon brought them home and married them. This was to disguise the sin as acceptable behavior.

- ✦ **Pride**. Many of Solomon's foreign wives were the daughters of tributary chiefs, given as gifts to Solomon. To turn them away might be offensive or cause a problem with a political ally. Pride was a major factor in Solomon's decision to bring so many women into his home. Ironically, it was Solomon himself who penned Proverbs 16:18, which warns, "Pride goes before destruction, and a haughty spirit before a fall."

- ✦ **Overconfidence**. Solomon was a wise man, but he may have been so confident in his knowledge and abilities that he thought he was invincible. He treated the women as possessions and believed he controlled them. There is definitely something wrong with anyone believing the lie that he has his life all together and nothing can go wrong. Second

Peter 3:17 says, "You therefore, beloved, since you know this beforehand, beware lest you also fall from your own steadfastness, being led away with the error of the wicked" (emphasis added). There are many other scriptures with the words *beware, guard, watch, be sober and vigilant,* and *awake.*

- **Power**. Solomon was king. Everyone in Israel bowed to him, catered to him, and obeyed his every wish. He probably got caught up in who really owned the power of the kingdom of Israel. Can't you hear him saying to himself, "God is talking to those lesser men. I am the king. I am sure He understands that I can handle these women"? Yet Psalm 62:11 reminds us, "Power belongs to God."

These strong emotional attachments, along with the sin in Solomon's life, brought about bad choices.

Do any of Solomon's destructive attitudes (pride, lust, power, overconfidence, justification by works, reasoning judgments, etc.) reside in you?

Always bear in mind that your own resolution to succeed is more important than any one thing.

—Abraham Lincoln

What is the ONE THING you can do to rid yourself of this attitude?

"I Can Control When I Stop"

And he had seven hundred wives, princesses, and three hundred concubines; and his wives turned away his heart. **—1 Kings 11:3**

What a sad verse! Solomon has been called one of the wisest men who ever lived. He wrote the book of Proverbs, which is often called the "Book of Wisdom." But he made some really dumb choices in his life. He disobeyed God's direct command not just once but one thousand times as he brought foreign women into his home, each with a foreign god. The first time, he may have been broad and boastful and sure, but soon he lost all self-control and simply could not stop.

Solomon might have begun by thinking, *I will change my pagan wives, and they will worship my God.* Today, we call that "missionary dating." A student may think, *I'll date that lost person just once so that I can share Christ with him (or her)*. But most of the time, your non-Christian date shares habits with you instead.

GROUP DISCUSSION

How was the nation of Israel affected by King Solomon's choices?

How is my circle of influence affected by my *reasoning*?

Is it possible to make a personal immoral choice without affecting others?

diffuse (di FYOOZ): to pour out and permit or cause to spread freely; to extend, scatter

In 2 Corinthians 10:5, the apostle Paul tells us that we are to use our spiritual weapons for "casting down arguments and every high thing that exalts itself against the knowledge of God, bringing every thought into captivity to the obedience of Christ."

This is an interesting verse. Paul tells us to get rid of arguments—that is, imagination and reasoning that we might use to defend sin against what we know is already true and right. We cannot just make stuff up in order to customize a type of Christian lifestyle.

We can control our choices while they are just thoughts. However, if we don't "bring every thought into captivity," we soon learn to tolerate sinful thoughts. It's not long before we justify them so that the guilt will feel lessened. The resulting emotions lead us to continue lowering our standards and running to places and people we would have once run from.

Is there a particular thought pattern that you believe the Lord would want you to change? What Scripture comes to mind that could help you to replace that thought with an absolute truth?

If you don't know one, ask a friend or teacher for help. They'll be happy to join with you in this positive step of growth in your life.

GROUP DISCUSSION

Some students may reason that since Jesus said that lusting is committing adultery in the heart (Matthew 5:28), it wouldn't be any worse to go "all the way." How would you respond to such reasoning?

According to 2 Corinthians 10:5, "every thought" has to be captured and brought into obedience, including our *intentions.* Solomon prided himself in following the Lord and in building His temple, but in his private world he did not follow the Lord with his whole heart. The once great King Solomon, who thought he had all power and control, now found himself in bondage to the things he never thought possible.

First Kings 11:4 tells us the sad outcome of Solomon's poor choices: "When Solomon was old … his wives turned his heart after other gods; and his heart was not loyal to the LORD his God, as was the heart of his father David." Whether it is a momentary bad choice or a series of bad choices throughout a lifetime, we destroy ourselves when we start to imagine and reason outside of the black and white teachings of God's Word.

GROUP DISCUSSION

How do I share the love of Christ without tolerating "gray" behavior?

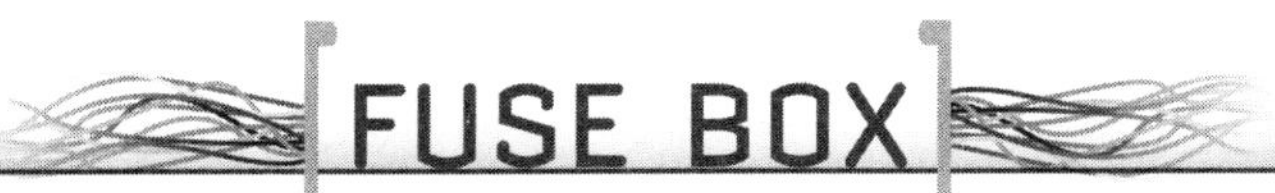

Throw out arguments, reasoning, and imagination about justifying sin. Capture every thought and intention into obedience to God's Word.

PRIVATE WORLD DEVOTIONS

MONDAY: See it. Read the surrounding passages or chapter for the Key Scripture so that you can get an understanding of the background and context. This helps you to really ***see*** the verse.

TUESDAY: Hear it. Read the daily Key Scripture and/or surrounding passage out loud, putting your name in, if applicable. For example, John *can do all things through Christ. Thieves have come to destroy* John, *but Jesus has come that* John *might have eternal life.*

WEDNESDAY: Write it. Write the verse and then what it says about:

- ***Others:*** Respond, serve, and love as Jesus would.
- ***Me:*** Specific attitudes, choices, or habits.
- ***God:*** His love, mercy, holiness, peace, joy, etc.

PRIVATE WORLD JOURNAL

I am grateful for—I praise you for—I am feeling—I am thinking—I need help with

PRIVATE WORLD DEVOTIONS *(Continued)*

THURSDAY: Memorize it. Take the verse with you—write it on a card or put it in your phone, iPod, or PDA. Go over it throughout the day so that it begins to *live* in your heart and mind.

FRIDAY: Pray it. Personalize the verse as you pray for yourself or for others or in praise to God. To pray is literally "to think about." Try thinking out loud or writing in your **PRIVATE WORLD JOURNAL.**

SATURDAY: Share it. Ask the Lord to bring someone to mind or in your path today who needs good news. Don't be shy—just let it out! Whether you IM, write, text, tell, or send it, the joy of God's Word will flow from your heart into theirs.

PRAYER REQUESTS

Date	Name	Need	Answer

PRIVATE WORLD JOURNAL

I am grateful for—I praise you for—I am feeling—I am thinking—I need help with

NOTES

CHAPTER 5

MENTAL FLOSS

KEY SCRIPTURE

Be sober, be vigilant; because your adversary the devil walks about like a roaring lion seeking whom he may devour.

—1 Peter 5:8

COULD THIS BE YOU?

Knowing the danger involved, more than twenty-four thousand KBR employees and subcontractors worked in the Kuwait-Iraq region in 2004.[1] Then on April 9, tragedy struck. While driving a truck for Halliburton Corporation in Iraq, Thomas Hamill's convoy was suddenly ambushed.[2] Four of the convoy members were found dead; three were missing. Thomas was taken captive and held hostage until he escaped and connected with U.S. troops on May 2, 2004.[3]

Thomas Hamill described his experience and passion to escape this way: "Well, the ambush was really horrific … the mental stress from not knowing from one day to the next whether they were going to kill me."

Thomas remembered the Word of God he had hidden in his heart, and he waited on God. Remembering the promises he had learned growing up, Thomas prayed. "I asked the Lord to find a time and a place and a day in the future. And that Sunday morning he had that day picked out. And that was the day I bounded for freedom."[4]

Opportunity may knock only once, but temptation leans on the doorbell.
—Author Unknown

What you remember from your youth will make or break you in time of stress.

WHY KNOW IT?

- ✦ 64 percent of all shows include sexual content, and only 15 percent mention waiting, protection, and consequences.[5]
- ✦ Nearly 50 percent of U.S. jail and prison inmates were under the influence of alcohol at the time of their offense, and many report not remembering the crime they committed because they were high at the time.[6]

transfuse (trans FYOOZ): to cause to pass from one to another; transmit

Reading the Word of God is vital; it gives us God's viewpoint about our lives. If you are a believer, Jesus Christ lives in you. When you go to the Bible for help and guidance, the Spirit of God connects with the Word of God, and there is synergy for your life. These two are meant to work together.

When it comes to flossing out old ways of thinking, reading the Word of God is our most potent weapon. Scripture is the perfect agent to get into those hard-to-reach places and clean out the destructive thoughts that decay or weaken our strength to become all that God wants for us.

The word of God is living and powerful, and sharper than any two-edged sword, piercing even to the division of soul and spirit, and of joints and marrow, and is a discerner of the thoughts and intents of the heart. **—Hebrews 4:12**

One Bible commentary explains Hebrews 4:12 like this: "The Word of God is living, powerful, and sharper than any two-edged sword, piercing even to the division of soul and spirit, and of joints and marrow. It is a discerner of the thoughts and intents of the heart. This Word is alive and has energetic power to transform. It is able to enter into the soul and spirit, and affect both eternal and everyday life. By piercing the joints and the marrow it directs both actions and feelings. There is no hiding from its power because it is capable of judging motive and intentions."[7] Nothing can stop the power of God's living Word—except for not using it.

infuse (in FYOOZ): to cause to be permeated with something (as a principle or quality) that alters usually for the better

In the world of very real evil, there is a very real devil, and his name is Satan. He walks about, 1 Peter 5:8 says, "like a roaring lion, seeking whom he may devour." Destruction is his intention and temptation is his sport. He enjoys it.

Jesus faced Satan head-on, and He gave us the first-person account in His Word that we might learn how to win.

The Antidote to Temptation

- Scripture is not one of the possible antidotes to temptation; *it is the only effective antidote to temptation.*
- Scripture dilutes the effects of temptation on our minds as we are brought into a sharp contrast of distorted truth and absolute truth.

If you haven't done it yet, start today to plan a time of Scripture memorization so that you are ready for whatever temptation Satan throws at you. If you are already memorizing, double your study time at least twice this week.

Jesus Overcomes Temptation with Scripture

Then Jesus was led up by the Spirit into the wilderness to be tempted by the devil. And when He had fasted forty days and forty nights, afterward He was hungry. Now when the tempter came to Him, he said, "If You are the Son of God, command that these stones become bread." But He answered and said, "It is written, 'Man shall not live by bread alone, but by every word that proceeds from the mouth of God.'" Then the devil took Him up into the holy city, set Him on the pinnacle of the temple, and said to Him, "If You are the Son of God, throw Yourself down. For it is written: 'He shall give His angels charge over you,' and, 'In their hands they shall bear you up, Lest you dash your foot against a stone.'" Jesus said to him, "It is written again, 'You shall not tempt the Lord your God.'" Again, the devil took Him up on an exceedingly high mountain, and showed Him all the kingdoms of the world and their glory. And he said to Him, "All these things I will give You if You will fall down and worship me." Then Jesus said to him, "Away with you, Satan! For it is written, 'You shall worship the Lord your God, and Him only you shall serve.'" **—Matthew 4:1–10**

1. The first test Jesus faced pertained to the matter of the *Father-Son relationship*. Satan thought that since Jesus was the Son, perhaps He could be persuaded to act independently of the Father.[8]

2. The second test by Satan appealed to *personal popularity*. This test built on the first, for if Jesus is the Son of God and the Messiah, nothing can harm Him. So Satan took Jesus to the highest point of the temple and said, in essence, "Why don't You do what the people are expecting and make some marvelous display? After all, the Scripture says God's angels will protect You, and You won't even hurt a foot as You come down." Satan may have thought that if Jesus could quote Scripture to him, he could quote it too.[9]

3. Satan's third and final test related to *God's plan for Jesus*. Satan showed Jesus the kingdoms of the world and all their splendor. His goal was to change Jesus from a heavenly-minded life and the perfect will of God to an earthly-minded life.

Every time you are tempted, it's an opportunity for God to lead you past the obstacle and into further personal transformation.

GROUP DISCUSSION

Can you think of a time when you were tempted but said no? How did that make you feel (good, bad, regretful, happy, etc.)?

When we choose to listen to destructive thoughts, we become depressed. But when we choose to replace those destructive thoughts with God's thoughts, we become stronger and more useable to God.

ASK YOURSELF

Whenever you are in doubt over temptation, ask yourself:

- ✦ Will my choice honor the Lord?
- ✦ Will I be proud of my choice?
- ✦ Would I feel good if my decision were published in the paper?
- ✦ What if my family knew about it?

diffuse (di FYOOZ): to pour out and permit or cause to spread freely; to extend, scatter

Temptation Is a Battle over Self-Control
Jesus refused to give in to any part of Satan's request because He knew that it would not stop there. Every temptation has a friend. Every choice has a consequence.

The Absolute Truth
One of Satan's weapons against us is to bring doubt on the absolute truth of God's Word.

- ✦ Satan likes to ask, "Does the Bible really say that? Are you sure? But isn't this a different situation?"
- ✦ Using just part of a verse or adding in an opinion is another favorite. Satan tried this with Eve and won when he said, "Did God really say that? Are you sure?"
- ✦ The bottom line is that Satan wants you to deny that God is God and to make choices based on emotions. "This feels right" has broken more relationships and caused more pain than perhaps any other excuse.

Satan understands that when you make a bad choice, you will probably lead others to do the same. And the more influential a leader you are, the greater number of people you will take with you.

The priority in Jesus's life is and was the truth of God's Word. He could have argued, used wisdom, or discussed the situation with Satan, but He chose the best and only defense. He simply said, "It is written," as He quoted from the Old Testament. Notice He didn't say, "It has been said" or, "I think it says somewhere." No, He knew the Scriptures. He said, "It is written." Once the Word is written, it will never be changed, and Jesus used the power of that to respond to Satan's tests.

A Christian doesn't hesistate to say, "It is written." What verse or passage of Scripture do you depend on in times of temptation? Write it here:

In order for the Word of God to work as a defense in your life, you have to know it. Five- or ten-minute devotionals aren't enough to let the Word of God become an essential part of your life. Jesus wants us to live by it, be filled by it, and exist by it. Jesus didn't tell Satan, "Let me look that up." He already knew the Scripture!

The Agent of Transformation

After Jesus's forty days of temptation by Satan were over, the Bible tells us, "Then the devil left Him, and behold, angels came and ministered to Him (Matthew 4:11).

Victory! Satan left, and angels came. What a party that must have been! They probably brought food, gave Jesus high fives, and sang praise songs with Him for a while.

- ✦ In the moment, temptation appears to fill a need—either of the flesh or of the spirit. But in the end, it leaves guilt and shame.
- ✦ When you say no to temptation and walk away strong, you are filled with joy, which is the exact opposite of guilt and shame.
- ✦ Each time you give in to temptation, giving in gets easier.
- ✦ Each time you walk away from temptation, you get stronger.

God is in the process of transforming you into the image of Christ. *Transformation* is not a special-effects movie term. It's the term God used when He said, "Be transformed by the renewing of your mind" (2 Corinthians 12:2).

CONTRAST

Truth	*Emotion*
God has forgiven you.	"I don't *feel* forgiven.
God knows your heart.	"No one understands me."
God has a plan for your life.	"I'm a nobody."

- ✦ Emotions are real, but they are not always right.
- ✦ When truth is introduced into a life that has been led by emotions, there is a fight.

When emotions are the lenses through which we view everything, it's impossible for us to get an accurate read on anything. The fight for truth is to reverse the emotional control. When God's Word is planted in your mind, it will renew your habits, actions, and attitudes.

Focus on knowing the Word and being able to say, "It is written." This is not so that you can confront and judge others, but so that you can offer them comfort and strength.

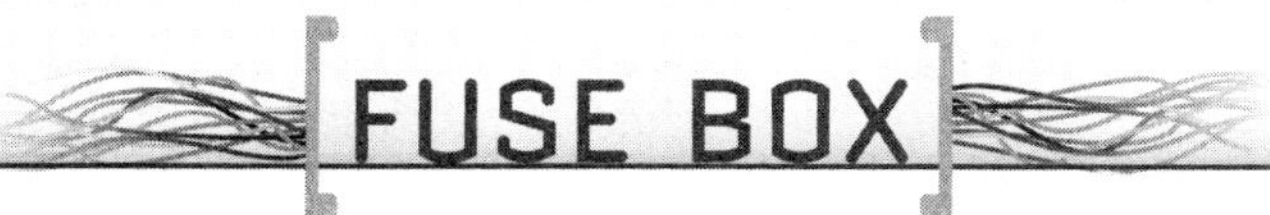

The battle for good choices is won or lost in the theatre of your mind.

However, when He, the Spirit of truth, has come, He will guide you into all truth; for He will not speak on His own authority, but whatever He hears He will speak; and He will tell you things to come.

—John 16:13

PRIVATE WORLD DEVOTIONS

MONDAY: See it. Read the surrounding passages or chapter for the Key Scripture so that you can get an understanding of the background and context. This helps you to really ***see*** the verse.

TUESDAY: Hear it. Read the daily Key Scripture and/or surrounding passage out loud, putting your name in, if applicable. For example, John *can do all things through Christ. Thieves have come to destroy* John, *but Jesus has come that* John *might have eternal life.*

WEDNESDAY: Write it. Write the verse and then what it says about:

- ***Others:*** Respond, serve, and love as Jesus would.
- ***Me:*** Specific attitudes, choices, or habits.
- ***God:*** His love, mercy, holiness, peace, joy, etc.

PRIVATE WORLD JOURNAL

I am grateful for—I praise you for—I am feeling—I am thinking—I need help with

PRIVATE WORLD DEVOTIONS *(Continued)*

THURSDAY: Memorize it. Take the verse with you—write it on a card or put it in your phone, iPod, or PDA. Go over it throughout the day so that it begins to *live* in your heart and mind.

FRIDAY: Pray it. Personalize the verse as you pray for yourself or for others or in praise to God. To pray is literally "to think about." Try thinking out loud or writing in your **PRIVATE WORLD JOURNAL.**

SATURDAY: Share it. Ask the Lord to bring someone to mind or in your path today who needs good news. Don't be shy—just let it out! Whether you IM, write, text, tell, or send it, the joy of God's Word will flow from your heart into theirs.

PRAYER REQUESTS

Date	Name	Need	Answer

PRIVATE WORLD JOURNAL

I am grateful for—I praise you for—I am feeling—I am thinking—I need help with

NOTES

CHAPTER 6

THE PERSON YOU WANT TO BE WITH

KEY SCRIPTURE

Who may ascend into the hill of the LORD? Or who may stand in His holy place? He who has clean hands and a pure heart, Who has not lifted up his soul to an idol, Nor sworn deceitfully. He shall receive blessing from the LORD, And righteousness from the God of his salvation.

—Psalm 24:3–5

COULD THIS BE YOU?

One day while working in the university office, Julie was asked to phone a list of twenty students and tell them that their exam for that Friday had been cancelled. It was an easy task, completed in just two hours.

For I am the LORD who brings you up out of the land of Egypt, to be your God. You shall therefore be holy, for I am holy.

—Leviticus 11:45

Friday came and she was ready for the history test, but there was no one else in the room when she arrived. After a few minutes of sitting by herself, she went to the department office to find out what was going on. The teacher's assistant working behind the desk informed her that the class had been canceled, and she should have received a call from someone. "Maybe the girl who was calling people wasn't able to get in touch with you."

Suddenly, Julie felt really dumb as she realized what had happened. She'd been in such a hurry the day she received the list of names to call that she didn't realize that all these people were from her history class. She'd had no problem telling everyone else about the schedule change, but she didn't think about changing her own schedule.

Have you ever noticed how easy it is to point out everyone else's flaws or possible improvements without ever seeing any of your own? It happens to all of us.

WHY KNOW IT?

- ✦ There are almost 4 million Web sites available that reference "on-line" dating for teens.[1]

transfuse (trans FYOOZ): to cause to pass from one to another; transmit

Students sometimes say they have a hard time making friends.

- ✦ Is it easier to find people you don't want to be with than it is to make friendships with the kind of people you do want to be with?

✦ Is it easier to point out what others need to do to change than to think about what kind of friend you would make?

✦ What about the people who are looking at you? What do they see? Are you the kind of person you would want to be with?

The process begins on the inside. Becoming the kind of person you want to be is not as easy as swallowing a pill or getting a shot. You can't go to sleep wishing and wake up with a new personality. It's a little more detailed, and it's full of adventure. God remakes us from the inside out.

Who may ascend into the hill of the LORD*? Or who may stand in His holy place? He who has clean hands and a pure heart, who has not lifted up his soul to an idol, nor sworn deceitfully. He shall receive blessing from the* LORD*, and righteousness from the God of his salvation.* **—Psalm 24:3–5**

In this psalm, David asks the right question: "Lord, what's a guy have to do to be able to hang out with You?" God answered, "Have clean hands and a pure heart."

- ✦ *Clean hands* refer to right actions.
- ✦ *A pure heart* refers to a right attitude and will.

Anytime we want to get close to the Lord, we begin by asking, "Lord, what does it take?" His answer is always "clean hands and pure heart," but it will be specific to your behavior and thought life. Those who strive to have a pure heart want to commune with God. To do this, they actively pursue being inwardly as pure as they appear to be outwardly.

infuse (in FYOOZ): to cause to be permeated with something (as a principle or quality) that alters usually for the better

Psalm 24 tells us how to be a person people want to be with. It just so happens to be the person God wants to be with as well!

The person you want to be with has:

1. The moral attributes of God
2. A solid foundation of beliefs
3. Valued relationships with God and man

The Moral Attributes of God

Only you and God know the areas of your life that need to be dealt with. As you learn more about the moral character of God, you will see your own character in a new way.

Holiness. David is thinking upward when he asks, "Who can go up to the hill of the Lord?" He understands that to be with God requires getting away from the noise of the world and separating himself to hear and be in the Lord's presence.

Only God is holy. But Scripture commands us to "be holy," which means that we:

- ✦ continually conform to the image of God;
- ✦ live by His absolute truth;
- ✦ desire nothing less than God's perfect will for our lives.

Conforming to the holiness of God is a personal journey. When a person is serious about this, he or she develops a peaceful character and becomes the kind of person that others are drawn to.

Choose all that apply to you. Do you have:

_________ The moral attributes of God

_________ A solid foundation of beliefs

_________ Valued relationships with God and man

If you truly desire to be a person others want to be with, what changes would you need to make in your current lifestyle?

Lead me, O Lord, in Your righteousness because of my enemies; Make Your way straight before my face.
—Psalm 5:8

Righteousness. God hates sin, but He loves the sinner. When we accept righteousness into our lives:

- ✦ we allow God to act in and through our lives;
- ✦ it changes who we are and why we do what we do;
- ✦ we join God in hating evil and loving the sinner;
- ✦ the blueprint of God's righteousness becomes engraved on our hearts.

GROUP DISCUSSION

What turns you off about potential friends? Are you guilty of the same?

Goodness. Ephesians 5:9 tells us that "the fruit of the Spirit is in all goodness." It is God's character to do good in every situation. Goodness:

- ✦ brings out the good in people;
- ✦ promotes moral actions that are favorable for others;
- ✦ causes us to do the right thing regardless of the way we've been treated.

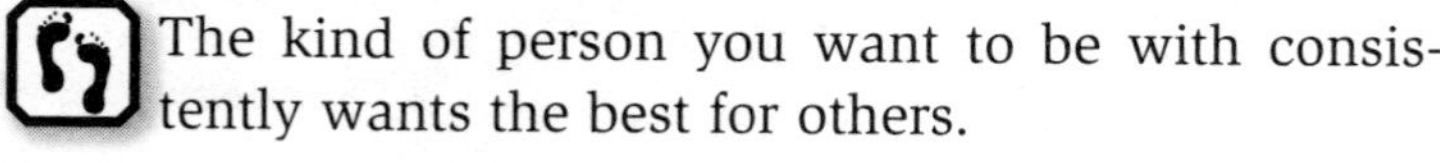

The kind of person you want to be with consistently wants the best for others.

Truth. Truth is the solid ground we stand on regardless of opinion, trouble, or circumstance. Every day, talk shows compete for audiences as they debate every opinion, piece of news, and real and imagined information. God's Word is absolute truth.

- ✦ For every question, doubt, or decision, God's Word has an answer that will not change whether others believe or whether you believe it.
- ✦ Truth is not relative; it stands when everything falls.

As long as you continue to choose your own truth, you limit yourself to only what you are able to discover and understand, instead of the abundance God has to offer.

Humility. People who are humble don't think less of themselves; they just think about themselves less. As Philippians 2:3 says, "Let nothing be done through selfish ambition or conceit, but in lowliness of mind let each esteem others better than himself."

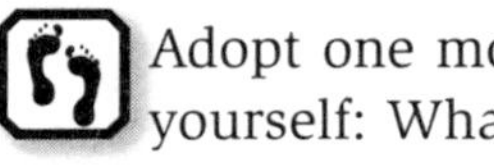

Adopt one moral attribute of God listed above for yourself: What is it?

The important issue is not to find the right person, but to be the right person.
—Greg Laurie

What is the ONE THING you could do this week to develop that attribute?

____

____

____

____

diffuse (di FYOOZ): to pour out and permit or cause to spread freely; to extend, scatter

A Solid Foundation of Beliefs

We need a generation of students who are more committed to the issue of purity according to God's character than they are their own rights.

 Personal conviction is:

- ✦ what keeps everything inside from crumbling;
- ✦ the greatest safeguard you have;
- ✦ the means by which God directs you;
- ✦ the measurement of choosing right and wrong.

What do you know to be true? Write the top three truths you depend on:

1. ______________________________
2. ______________________________
3. ______________________________

Valued Relationships with God and Man
Intimacy with God makes it possible to walk past temptation, teaches us how to love others, and helps us to love purity.

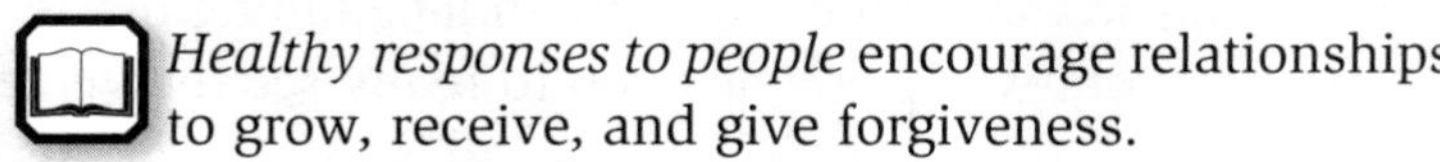

Healthy responses to people encourage relationships to grow, receive, and give forgiveness.

Commitment to a local church provides spiritual friendships, which are essential. Be a part of corporate worship; be a part of a kingdom team.

Do you display characteristics that would make people want to partner with you?

What's worse than having no Christian friends is having Christian friends who compromise their moral integrity.

Jesus said to him, "I am the way, the truth, and the life. No one comes to the Father except through Me."
—John 14:6

PRIVATE WORLD DEVOTIONS

MONDAY: See it. Read the surrounding passages or chapter for the Key Scripture so that you can get an understanding of the background and context. This helps you to really ***see*** the verse.

TUESDAY: Hear it. Read the daily Key Scripture and/or surrounding passage out loud, putting your name in, if applicable. For example, John *can do all things through Christ. Thieves have come to destroy* John, *but Jesus has come that* John *might have eternal life.*

WEDNESDAY: Write it. Write the verse and then what it says about:

- ***Others:*** Respond, serve, and love as Jesus would.
- ***Me:*** Specific attitudes, choices, or habits.
- ***God:*** His love, mercy, holiness, peace, joy, etc.

PRIVATE WORLD JOURNAL

I am grateful for—I praise you for—I am feeling—I am thinking—I need help with

PRIVATE WORLD DEVOTIONS *(Continued)*

THURSDAY: Memorize it. Take the verse with you—write it on a card or put it in your phone, iPod, or PDA. Go over it throughout the day so that it begins to *live* in your heart and mind.

FRIDAY: Pray it. Personalize the verse as you pray for yourself or for others or in praise to God. To pray is literally "to think about." Try thinking out loud or writing in your **PRIVATE WORLD JOURNAL.**

SATURDAY: Share it. Ask the Lord to bring someone to mind or in your path today who needs good news. Don't be shy—just let it out! Whether you IM, write, text, tell, or send it, the joy of God's Word will flow from your heart into theirs.

PRAYER REQUESTS

Date	Name	Need	Answer

PRIVATE WORLD JOURNAL

I am grateful for—I praise you for—I am feeling—I am thinking—I need help with

NOTES

CHAPTER 7

IT MATTERS HOW YOU LIVE

KEY SCRIPTURE

Observe and obey all these words which I command you, that it may go well with you and your children after you forever, when you do what is good and right in the sight of the LORD your God.

—Deuteronomy 12:28

COULD THIS BE YOU?

Growing up as the daughter of an African-American sharecropper in Alabama during the 1950s was not exactly easy living for Janice Rogers Brown.[1] Segregation was a heated issue, and she learned firsthand what it was like to be shut out—not being allowed or welcome in certain places because of her skin color.

Janice was active in her church, and her family taught her the importance of being part of a church home. Inspired as a teen by a lawyer named Fred Gray, Janice decided she would become a lawyer.[2] She graduated from California State University and then went on to receive her JD from UCLA.

> I am only one; but still I am one. I cannot do everything, but still I can do something; I will not refuse to do something I can do.
>
> —Helen Keller

Janice remembered the faith of her youth as she served people through the law. In one speech, she expressed, "These are perilous times for people of faith, not in the sense that we are going to lose our lives, but in the sense that it will cost you something if you are a person of faith who stands up for what you believe in, and say those things out loud."[3]

As a public servant, Janice Brown knows about having her beliefs questioned on a very public level. After two years of debate about her reputation, in July 2005 she was finally confirmed by the U.S. Senate to serve on the U.S. Court of Appeals for the District of Columbia Circuit.[4] Janice Brown has learned that a successful future is created one day at a time and that a reputation of consistency opens the next door and the next in life.

WHY KNOW IT?

- ✦ 51 percent of church members feel that the leadership in their congregation makes them enthusiastic about the future.[5]

transfuse (trans FYOOZ): to cause to pass from one to another; transmit

It matters how you live, all the time. Most students are so concerned about the pressures and confusion of today that they don't stop to think about the future. What you do today will indeed purchase your tomorrows.

For we do not have a High Priest who cannot sympathize with our weaknesses, but was in all points tempted as we are, yet without sin. **—Hebrews 4:15**

The moment Adam and Eve sinned, God promised a sacrifice to pay for that sin. His intention was that He Himself would leave the riches of heaven, come to the poverty of earth, be tempted as we are tempted, and experience life as we would. To accomplish this, He needed human partners—Joseph and Mary.

God is still looking for men and women whom He can use for His purposes. Although He loves each of us equally, we are chosen for service based on the purity of our hearts and our willingness to serve.

infuse (in FYOOZ): to cause to be permeated with something (as a principle or quality) that alters usually for the better

Joseph was a man whom God used for His purposes. Very little is written in Scripture about him, but the few words speak volumes about his character.

As we read about Joseph, we learn that the man or woman God selects for His service has four essential character traits:

1. Listens and responds to instruction
2. Rules over instinct
3. Responds immediately
4. Has a reputation of excellence

Obey: to hear, give attention to, and consent.

Listens and Responds to Instruction

Then Joseph, being aroused from sleep, did as the angel of the Lord commanded him and took to him his wife. —**Matthew 1:24**

Now when they had departed, behold, an angel of the Lord appeared to Joseph in a dream, saying, "Arise, take the young Child and His mother, flee to Egypt, and stay there until I bring you word; for Herod will seek the young Child to destroy Him." When he arose, he took the young Child and His mother by night and departed for Egypt. —**Matthew 2:13–14**

Joseph was probably afraid to go to sleep at night! Twice during sleep, the Lord spoke to him, requiring immediate obedience and personal sacrifice.

- ✦ God chose Joseph because He knew what was in his heart.
- ✦ He knew that Joseph would respond in obedience. This was too big a deal to take a chance on a "maybe" kind of guy. He had to be sure.
- ✦ He knew that Joseph would take the request and the responsibility to serve seriously.
- ✦ The Lord didn't have to catch Joseph in a good mood or make sure he was spiritually ready.
- ✦ Joseph didn't debate, didn't check with friends, and didn't tell the Lord about how tired he was. He heard. He got up and went.

ASK YOURSELF

If the Lord was thinking of choosing you, how many of the character traits listed above would He be able to count on? Circle them.

If you are to be used of God, the first step is to practice listening. Get away from the Internet, the TV, the phone, and people. Be open to God speaking to you as you develop this habit, and He will.

- ✦ You cannot *respond* if you do not hear.
- ✦ You cannot *hear* if you are constantly surrounded by noise.

If I want God to bless my future, I have to be willing to listen in the present.

Rules Over Instinct

And (Joseph) did not know her till she had brought forth her firstborn Son. And he called His name Jesus. **—Matthew 1:25**

Personal purity is about personal sacrifice. It means that we are willing to be patient, make changes, serve others, and develop a personal intimacy with God.

Joseph took the challenge and made personal sacrifice his first choice. God told him to take Mary as his wife—but not to have sexual relations with her until after the baby was born. Can't you just see Joseph's face? *Baby? What baby?*

In other words, just do it! Honor God, and He will honor you.

For Joseph, obeying God through personal sacrifice meant:

- completely disrupting his life's plans;
- explaining to friends and family why he was doing something that seemed unreasonable;
- facing ridicule and gossip;
- losing friendships.

Can I be counted on to patiently and compassionately love those people whom God places in my care, even if it requires personal sacrifice?

Am I willing to pay a personal price to be used of God, or am I all talk?

It is easier to keep a reputation than it is to regain it.

Is there anything or anyone in my life I am not willing to give up (a relationship, a sport, club, activity, purchase, time, money, attitude, etc.)?

Joseph made personal sacrifice his first choice, and this allowed him to be used of God publicly. He made the choice to choose sacrifice over the easy life. He knew the wisdom of Proverbs 16:32, which says, "He who is slow to anger is better than the mighty, and he who rules his spirit than he who takes a city."

Responds Immediately

Christians want to know:

- ✦ How can I be used of God?
- ✦ How do I get in on the big adventure?
- ✦ What is God's plan for my life?

Many times, we are looking for the big thing—the mission trip, an opportunity to speak, or being chosen as a leader—but God is watching the small responses. Obedience in the basics is key.

GROUP DISCUSSION

What are some "small things" in which God might ask for obedience? (For example, excellence in your schoolwork, being respectful at home, having willingness to serve, being on time, obeying rules, etc.)

In Deuteronomy 12:28, God says, "Observe and obey all these words which I command you, that it may go well with you and your children after you forever, when you do what is good and right in the sight of the LORD your God."

Joseph learned that it was in the day in and day out that God chose him. Notice that each time God called, Joseph answered:

- ✦ "Joseph, being aroused from sleep, did as the angel commanded" (Matthew 1:24).
- ✦ "When he arose, he took the young Child ... and departed" (Matthew 2:14).

diffuse (di FYOOZ): to pour out and permit or cause to spread freely; to extend, scatter

Has a Reputation of Excellence
It is no little thing that Joseph was chosen to be the earthly father of the Son of God. He was chosen because of his reputation.

- ✦ He was tender and caring and respectful of women.
- ✦ He was dependable.
- ✦ He was committed to the Scripture.

Knowing that Christ was God in the flesh, we would have to believe that Joseph was a man who sought after holiness.

What ONE THING from the list above could you focus on becoming in reputation?

What is one specific action you could take this week in this area?

A leader obeys God without regard to conditions. What are you holding back on?

Your reputation is your most valuable possession. When people look for trustworthiness, do they look for you? When they search for dependability, do they call your name? You make the choice today to write your resume and bio. The way you walk is the way you'll be remembered.

Joseph's life reveals a model for establishing and maintaining personal purity. He found out that sacrifice can be costly. But when you pay the price by living in ways that matter, it pays off in huge dividends.

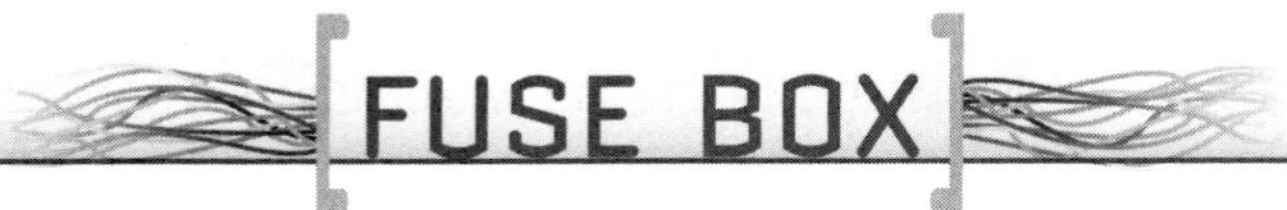

It matters how you live when you want your life to matter.

The conquest of ourselves, and our own unruly passions, requires more true wisdom, and a more steady, constant, and regular management, than the obtaining of a victory over the forces of an enemy.
—Matthew Henry

PRIVATE WORLD DEVOTIONS

MONDAY: See it. Read the surrounding passages or chapter for the Key Scripture so that you can get an understanding of the background and context. This helps you to really ***see*** the verse.

TUESDAY: Hear it. Read the daily Key Scripture and/or surrounding passage out loud, putting your name in, if applicable. For example, John *can do all things through Christ. Thieves have come to destroy* John, *but Jesus has come that* John *might have eternal life.*

WEDNESDAY: Write it. Write the verse and then what it says about:

- ***Others:*** Respond, serve, and love as Jesus would.
- ***Me:*** Specific attitudes, choices, or habits.
- ***God:*** His love, mercy, holiness, peace, joy, etc.

PRIVATE WORLD JOURNAL

I am grateful for—I praise you for—I am feeling—I am thinking—I need help with

PRIVATE WORLD DEVOTIONS *(Continued)*

THURSDAY: Memorize it. Take the verse with you—write it on a card or put it in your phone, iPod, or PDA. Go over it throughout the day so that it begins to *live* in your heart and mind.

FRIDAY: Pray it. Personalize the verse as you pray for yourself or for others or in praise to God. To pray is literally "to think about." Try thinking out loud or writing in your **PRIVATE WORLD JOURNAL.**

SATURDAY: Share it. Ask the Lord to bring someone to mind or in your path today who needs good news. Don't be shy—just let it out! Whether you IM, write, text, tell, or send it, the joy of God's Word will flow from your heart into theirs.

PRAYER REQUESTS

Date	Name	Need	Answer

PRIVATE WORLD JOURNAL

I am grateful for—I praise you for—I am feeling—I am thinking—I need help with

NOTES

CHAPTER 8

IT'S NEVER WRONG TO DO RIGHT

KEY SCRIPTURE

And the LORD said to Joshua, "Do not fear them, for I have delivered them into your hand, not a man of them shall stand before you."

—Joshua 10:8

COULD THIS BE YOU?

You see a tousled, dirty woman on the street with a baby or small child, holding out a hand in hopes of food or money, and your heart is touched. Maybe you drop in some coins or give a few dollars. We have so much; they have so little.

A few days later, you see the same woman, but this time she has a different baby. You learn from local storeowners that the lady isn't really homeless, and she uses her friends' children to evoke compassion and money from passers-by. You've been punked!

You gave money to someone who is able to work but instead uses children to make money. What do you do? Do you ask for your money back? Do you demand an explanation? Or do you believe that your actions were prompted by the love of Christ within you?

You may have made a mistake in trusting the woman, but you didn't make a mistake in obeying your heart.

WHY KNOW IT?

- ✦ 75 percent of high school students engage in serious cheating.[1]
- ✦ 50 percent of high school students have plagiarized work they found on the Internet.[2]
- ✦ 50 percent of high school students surveyed said they don't believe that copying questions and answers from a test is cheating.[3]

transfuse (trans FYOOZ): to cause to pass from one to another; transmit

The Internet has become a valuable resource for consumers and collectors. You can find amazing deals on authentic collectibles—or can you? Many of the so-called collectibles are actually being sold with deceptive language. They say enough to make you want to buy the products, but not enough to get themselves in trouble. An autograph might "appear to be genuine," or an item might be listed as "really old" instead of antique. It's a game of delicate deception meant to cause you to make a wrong decision.

Sometimes a bad decision is just about losing money, and that hurts your pride. But some bad decisions carry more serious consequences, such as:

- ✦ hurting a person's feelings,
- ✦ damaging a reputation, or
- ✦ leading a person down the wrong path.

But God has a way of using everything bad to do something good, if we work with Him.

[The Gibeonites] worked craftily, and went and pretended to be ambassadors. And they took old sacks on their donkeys, old wineskins torn and mended, old and patched sandals on their feet, and old garments on themselves; and all the bread of their provision was dry and moldy. And they went to Joshua, to the camp at Gilgal, and said to him and to the men of Israel, "We have come from a far country; now therefore, make a covenant with us." Then the men of Israel said "Perhaps you dwell among us; so how can we make a covenant with you?" But they said to Joshua, "We are your servants." And Joshua said to them, "Who are you, and where do you come from?" So they said to him: "From a very far country your servants have come, because of the name of the LORD your God; for we have heard of His fame, and all that He did in Egypt … Then the men of Israel took some of their provisions; but they did not ask counsel of the LORD. So Joshua made peace with them, and made a covenant with them to let them live; and the rulers of the congregation swore to them. **—Joshua 9:4–9, 14, 15**

Joshua spent his life learning to be God's man.

- ✦ He faithfully served under Moses,
- ✦ stayed positive when others complained,
- ✦ was full of courage in the face of adversity,
- ✦ was used of God as a great leader, and
- ✦ was well respected by the people as a leader.

So when the Gibeonites heard of Joshua's victories throughout the land, they were afraid. They appealed to Joshua's ego by saying, "We are your servants" (v. 8). They flattered him, and then they went in for the kill.

Joshua fell right into it. He had no idea that he had been punked.

infuse (in FYOOZ): to cause to be permeated with something (as a principle or quality) that alters usually for the better

Take Responsibility for the Error

And it happened at the end of three days, after they had made a covenant with them, that they heard that they were their neighbors who dwelt near them.... And all the congregation complained against the rulers. **—Joshua 9:16, 18**

The guys in the camp decided to check out the local neighbors and discovered that these guys were not from a far country, but just down the valley. As soon as Joshua heard about the deception, he realized what he had done: "The men of Israel took some of their provisions; but *they did not ask counsel of the Lord*" (v. 14; emphasis added). Ouch! Joshua knew his mistake.

Obviously, the Gibeonites lied. They deceived. *But Joshua made the wrong decision.* Now what should he do? Should he give in to the crowd and break his promise of peace?

He could have justified going back on his word to the Gibeonites. Or he could have started the blame game:

- "Why didn't you guys seek the counsel of the Lord?"
- "Look what you did!"

Bottom line: Joshua knew that he had fallen short in the leadership role. Ultimately, the decision was on his head. When the complaining started, Joshua had some decisions to make.

So he stepped up to the plate and took responsibility for his error.

God is calling for a generation of young adults who will follow Joshua's lead and take responsibility for their mistakes. He wants denial to stop and confession to start.

When we go into a situation without the counsel of God:

- *We set ourselves up to be punked.* We believe what we feel rather than trust what God says to be true. We put confidence in our judgment rather than in God's wisdom.
- *We bypass the check of the Holy Spirit in our hearts.* The men warned Joshua, but he didn't listen to them. Don't make the same mistake Joshua did! Listen to the godly people in your life who may be leading you to look more deeply at a situation.
- *We set ourselves up for constant struggle.* The Gibeonite situation did not go away. The Israelites and Gibeonites had to get along, work together, and be taken care of.
- *We detour the successful life God has for us.* All of a sudden, we find ourselves stopping to deal with a problem we never were meant to deal with in the first place. This happens when we date unbelievers and try to convince ourselves that it's OK.

Stay True to Your Promise and to the Word

And now, here we are, in your hands;
do with us as it seems good and right
to do to us. **—Joshua 9:25**

Joshua could have responded any way he wanted! This was an open invitation to retaliation. And his people would have supported him. In fact, you might say that the Gibeonites deserved it because of their lies and deception.

But Joshua was smart enough to know that when a leader makes a promise, a leader keeps a promise. In this case:

- ✦ Joshua's reputation depended on it.
- ✦ What the Gibeonites believed about the Hebrew God depended on it.
- ✦ This was Joshua's opportunity to show a different spirit.

Joshua was concerned about the testimony of God's character as shown through his decision. Retaliation over hurt didn't enter into the equation.

What would you have done in this situation? If you found out someone tricked you with lies and deception:

- ✦ How would you react?
- ✦ Would you keep your promise?
- ✦ Would you get angry and walk out?
- ✦ Would you take responsibility and work through the conflict?

Has someone tricked you with lies and deception?

What did you do?

I've learned that people will forget what you said, people will forget what you did, but people will never forget how you made them feel.
—Maya Angelou

What is ONE THING you would now do differently based on this lesson?

diffuse (di FYOOZ): to pour out and permit or cause to spread freely; to extend, scatter

Be Ready to Follow Through

All of this sounds OK so far, right? Joshua made the Gibeonites into slaves. That's not so bad. But what he didn't realize was that the people were now his responsibility:

Now it came to pass when Adoni-Zedek king of Jerusalem heard how ... the inhabitants of Gibeon had made peace with Israel and were among them, that they feared greatly, because Gibeon was a great city ... and all its men were mighty. Therefore Adoni-Zedek king of Jerusalem sent (word) ... saying, "Come up to me and help me, that we may attack Gibeon, for it has made peace with Joshua and with the children of Israel." Therefore the five kings of the Amorites, the king of Jerusalem, the king of Hebron, the king of Jarmuth, the king of Lachish, and the king of Eglon, gathered together and went up, they and all their armies, and camped before Gibeon and made war against it. **—Joshua 10:1–5**

Now Joshua had to keep his promise. These who were once strangers, now slaves, needed his help. How far does leadership have to go? When do you get to drop the responsibility? This was no easy task the Gibeonites were asking. They said to Joshua, "Do not forsake your servants; come up to us quickly, save us and help us, for all the kings of the Amorites who dwell in the mountains have gathered together against us" (v. 6).

Five kings and armies against one city—one city of liars and deceivers. (Those are the ones who usually get in trouble!) Who do they call? God's man, of course, because they know that God will come with him.

"Joshua, help!"

Don't you imagine that the children of Israel were reluctant to help these deceivers? There was major risk involved.

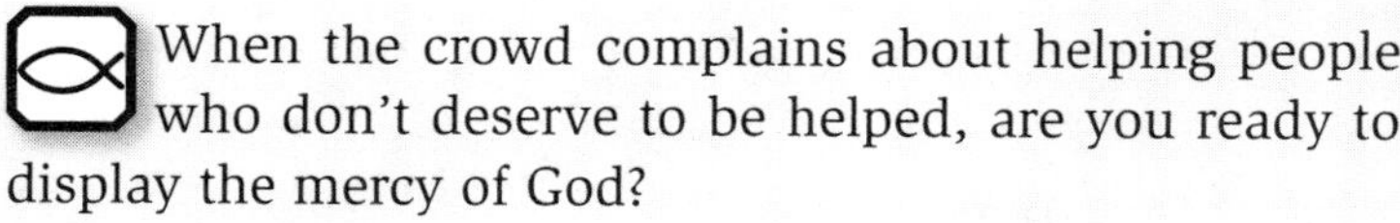

When the crowd complains about helping people who don't deserve to be helped, are you ready to display the mercy of God?

Take the Whole Counsel of God

This time, Joshua took the time to ask counsel of the Lord! And the Lord, in His infinite patience and love, answered Him. He told Joshua, "Do not fear them, for I have delivered them into your hand; not a man of them shall stand before you" (v. 8). This was a turning point for Joshua.

- ✦ He could correct his testimony by trusting God in a huge way.
- ✦ He could show the Gibeonites what faith in the living God could do.

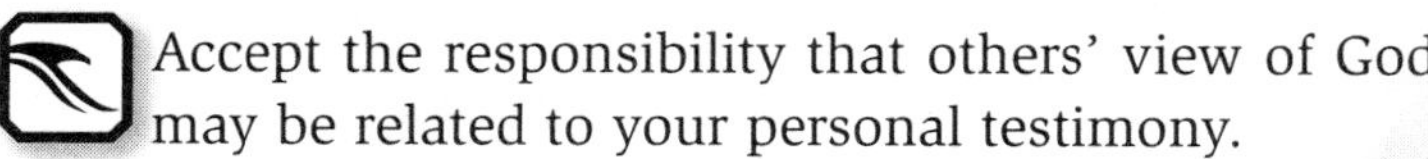

Accept the responsibility that others' view of God may be related to your personal testimony.

Five armies, one city, and Joshua and the Israelites. The Lord said, "It's done. Go." Through this situation, Joshua deepened his walk with God so much that when He said, "Go," Joshua got up and went.

Joshua 10:8–11 describes how Joshua's obedience was rewarded:

Joshua therefore came upon them suddenly, having marched all night from Gilgal. So the LORD routed them before Israel, killed them with a great slaughter at Gibeon, chased them along the road that goes to Beth Horon, and struck them down as far as Azekah and Makkedah.

And it happened, as they fled before Israel and were on the descent of Beth Horon, that the LORD cast down large hailstones from heaven on them as far as Azekah, and they died. There were more who died from the hailstones than the children of Israel killed with the sword.

Joshua learned that God is in a partnership with us.

- ✦ *He encouraged Joshua:* "I have delivered them into your hand" (v. 8).
- ✦ *He planned ahead:* "Not a man of them shall stand" (v. 8).
- ✦ *He walked beside:* "The LORD cast down large hailstones from heaven" (v. 11)
- ✦ *He gave the victory:* "More ... died from the hailstones than the children of Israel killed" (v. 11).

There is no situation so bad that God can't make it good if you will choose to handle your wrong decisions in the right way.

God Forgives and Restores Us Completely

Yes, Joshua blew it. But God, in His amazing mercy, didn't hold it against him. Not only did God come alongside Joshua and give him the victory, but He did something for Joshua that has never been done before or since—He gave Joshua the miracle that he needed.

Joshua 10:12–14 records the day the sun stood still for Joshua to finish the battle:

Then Joshua spoke to the LORD in the day when the LORD delivered up the Amorites before the children of Israel, and he said in the sight of Israel: "Sun, stand still over Gibeon; and Moon, in the Valley of Aijalon." So the sun stood still, and the moon stopped, Till the

people had revenge upon their enemies... .
And there has been no day like that, before
it or after it, that the LORD heeded the voice
of a man; for the LORD fought for Israel.

Amazing! The Creator said, "You need more sunlight, Joshua? You got it!" And the sun literally held still long enough for the battle to end.

There is no excuse for bad choices or bad behavior. But this story illustrates the absolute personal nature of a relationship with God. He looked at Joshua's whole heart. He played back Joshua's years of faithfulness, and He said, "Let's put this behind us and move on." And, as only God can do, He brought His relationship with Joshua to a closer level than before.

Be ready to share with others about the God of second chances and the depth of His mercy. They will be excited to hear about it.

Who can you tell?

What will you say?

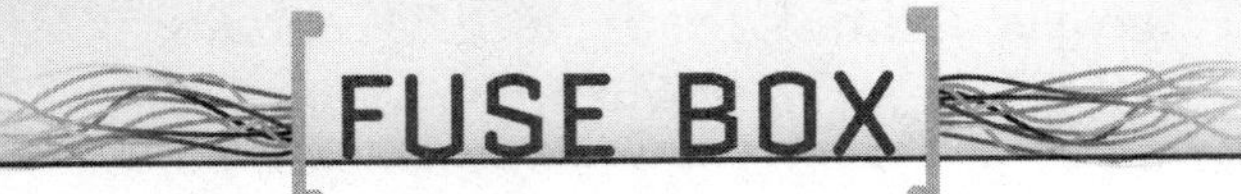

Taking responsibility for sin allows God to come in and bless our lives in amazing ways.

NOTES

PRIVATE WORLD DEVOTIONS

MONDAY: See it. Read the surrounding passages or chapter for the Key Scripture so that you can get an understanding of the background and context. This helps you to really ***see*** the verse.

TUESDAY: Hear it. Read the daily Key Scripture and/or surrounding passage out loud, putting your name in, if applicable. For example, <u>John</u> *can do all things through Christ. Thieves have come to destroy* <u>John</u>, *but Jesus has come that* <u>John</u> *might have eternal life.*

WEDNESDAY: Write it. Write the verse and then what it says about:

- ✦ ***Others:*** Respond, serve, and love as Jesus would.
- ✦ ***Me:*** Specific attitudes, choices, or habits.
- ✦ ***God:*** His love, mercy, holiness, peace, joy, etc.

PRIVATE WORLD JOURNAL

I am grateful for—I praise you for—I am feeling—I am thinking—I need help with

PRIVATE WORLD DEVOTIONS *(Continued)*

THURSDAY: Memorize it. Take the verse with you—write it on a card or put it in your phone, iPod, or PDA. Go over it throughout the day so that it begins to *live* in your heart and mind.

FRIDAY: Pray it. Personalize the verse as you pray for yourself or for others or in praise to God. To pray is literally "to think about." Try thinking out loud or writing in your **PRIVATE WORLD JOURNAL.**

SATURDAY: Share it. Ask the Lord to bring someone to mind or in your path today who needs good news. Don't be shy—just let it out! Whether you IM, write, text, tell, or send it, the joy of God's Word will flow from your heart into theirs.

PRAYER REQUESTS

Date	Name	Need	Answer

PRIVATE WORLD JOURNAL

I am grateful for—I praise you for—I am feeling—I am thinking—I need help with

NOTES

Notes

CHAPTER 1—MYTHS, LIES, AND FABRICATIONS ABOUT A PURE LIFE

1. Bob Minzesheimer, "Glass Glove Fits Cinderella Man," *USA Today*, (12 May 2005). http://www.usatoday.com/printedition/life/20050513/d_schaap13.art.htm (accessed 15 July 2005).
2. James J. Braddock, "The Man" http://www.jamesjbraddock.com/theman/ (accessed 15 July 2005).
3. Chris Matthews, "Russell Crowe Plays Hardball," MSNBC *Hardball* (10 June 2005). http://www.msnbc.msn.com/id/6448213/did/8170650 (accessed 15 July 2005).
4. Peter Heller, *"In This Corner . . . !": Forty-Two World Champions Tell Their Stories* (Cambridge, Mass.: Da Capo, 1994). http://www.murphsplace.com/crowe/braddock/own-words.html (accessed 15 July 2005).
5. Dale Buss, "Christian Teens, Not Very," *Wall Street Journal* (9 July 2004). http://www.opinionjournal.com/taste/?id = 110005335.
6. Ibid.

CHAPTER 2—PURITY FROM THE INSIDE OUT

1. Joel Stottrup, "Teen Rescues Woman from Lake," *Princeton (Minn.) Union-Eagle* (29 June 2005). www.unioneagle.com/2005/June/29rescue.html.
2. "Americans Draw Theological Beliefs from Diverse Points of View," The Barna Organization (8 October 2002). http://www.barna.org/FlexPage.aspx?Page = BarnaUpdate&BarnaUpdateID = 122 (accessed 13 July 2005).

CHAPTER 3—BULLETPROOFING YOUR LIFE

1. "Risking Your Life to Make a Ham and Cheese Sandwich," The Moderate Voice, http://www.themoderatevoice.com/posts/1108452045.shtml.

2. George Barna, "Teens Evaluate the Church-Based Ministry They Received As Children," 8 July 2003. http://www.barna.org/FlexPage.aspx?Page = BarnaUpdate&BarnaUpdateID = 143.

3. "Sex on TV: Content and Context," The Kaiser Family Foundation, 5 February 2001. http://www.kff.org/entmedia/loader.cfm?url = commonspot/security/getfile.cfm&PageID = 14210.

CHAPTER 4—SELF-DESTRUCTION

1. "Sexuality, Contraception, and the Media," American Academy of Pediatrics Committee on Public Education, January 2001. http://aappolicy.aappublications.org/cgi/content/full/pediatrics;107/1/191.

CHAPTER 5—MENTAL FLOSS

1. "Town Awaits Word on U.S. Civilian Kidnapped in Iraq," *USA Today* (11 April 2004). http://www.usatoday.com/news/world/2004-04-11-hostage_x.htm (accessed 15 July 2005).

2. "Hamill: Abuse at Iraqi Prison Affected Treatment," CNN (9 May 2004) http://www.cnn.com/2004/US/South/05/08/hamill.abuse (accessed 15 July 2005).

3. "Kidnapped U.S. Contractor Found Safe," CNN (2 May 2004) http://www.cnn.com/2004/WORLD/meast/05/02/iraq.main/ (accessed 15 July 2005).

4. "Transcript: Hamill Recounts 'Horrific' Ambush," The Crusader (5 September 2004) http://christian-patriot.blogspot.com/2004/05/transcript-hamill-recounts-horrific.html (accessed 15 July 2005).

5. "TV Sex Getting 'Safer,'" Kaiser Family Foundation. http://www.kff.org, 2003.

6. Data reported in *Catalyst*, National Crime Prevention Council 19, no. 7 (August 2000), based on research by the Bureau of Justice Statistics, the National Institute of Justice, the Center for Substance Abuse Prevention, and the Urban Institute and the Pacific Institute for Research and Evaluation.

7. Robert Jamieson, A. R. Fausset, and David Brown, *Commentary Critical and Explanatory on the Whole Bible.* Crosswalk. http://bible1.crosswalk.com/Commentaries/JamiesonFaussetBrown (accessed 14 July 2005).

8. J. F. Walvoord and R. B. Zuck, *The Bible Knowledge Commentary: An Exposition of the Scriptures* (Wheaton, Ill: Victor, 1983).
9. Ibid.

CHAPTER 6—THE PERSON YOU WANT TO BE WITH

1. Search conducted on www.google.com, September 20, 2005.

CHAPTER 7—IT MATTERS HOW YOU LIVE

1. David Brody, "Janice Rogers Brown: From Humble Beginnings to the Calif. High Court," CBN http://www.cbn.com/cbnnews/news/050520a.asp (accessed 15 July 2005).
2. Ibid.
3. Ibid.
4. "Justice Janice Rogers Brown Confirmed for Federal Appeals Court," Judicial Council of California (8 June 2005) http://www.courtinfo.ca.gov/presscenter/newsreleases/MEDIA08.PDF (accessed 15 July 2005).
5. Albert L. Winseman, "Ministering to a Divided Nation," The Gallup Organization (28 December 2004) http://www.gallup.com/poll/content/?ci=14455&pg=1 (accessed 13 July 2005).

CHAPTER 8—IT'S NEVER WRONG TO DO RIGHT

1. Alexander Rafael and Emily Anderson, "College Life 2.0," *Current* (Winter 2004). http://msnbc.msn.com/id/6596310/site/newsweek (accessed 13 July 2005).
2. Kathy Slobogin, "Survey: Many Students Say Cheating Is OK," CNN (5 April 2002).
3. Ibid.

ABOUT THE AUTHORS

Jay Strack, president and founder of Student Leadership University, is an inspiring and effective communicator, author, and minister. Acclaimed by leaders in the business world, religious affiliations, and education realms as a dynamic speaker, Jay has spoken to an estimated 15 million people in his 30 years of ministry. His versatile style has been presented across the country and in 22 countries, before government officials, corporate groups, numerous professional sports teams in the NFL, NBA, and MLB, to over 9,500 school assemblies, and at some 100 universities. Zig Ziglar calls Jay Strack "entertaining, but powerful, inspiring and informative."

David Edwards travels as a full-time speaker to over 500,000 students and adults each year, sharing from his heart about issues relevant to the Postmodern Generation. Regardless of the setting—schools, camps, retreats, or Sunday services—David's message is simple—discovering the importance of a Christ-centered lifestyle. David masterfully applies biblical truths to today's tough issues. Author of twelve books, David teaches a city-wide bible study for 1,600 students in Greenville, Texas, and is currently on the teaching team for 722 Bible Study in Atlanta, Georgia. You can find out more about David at www.davetown.com.

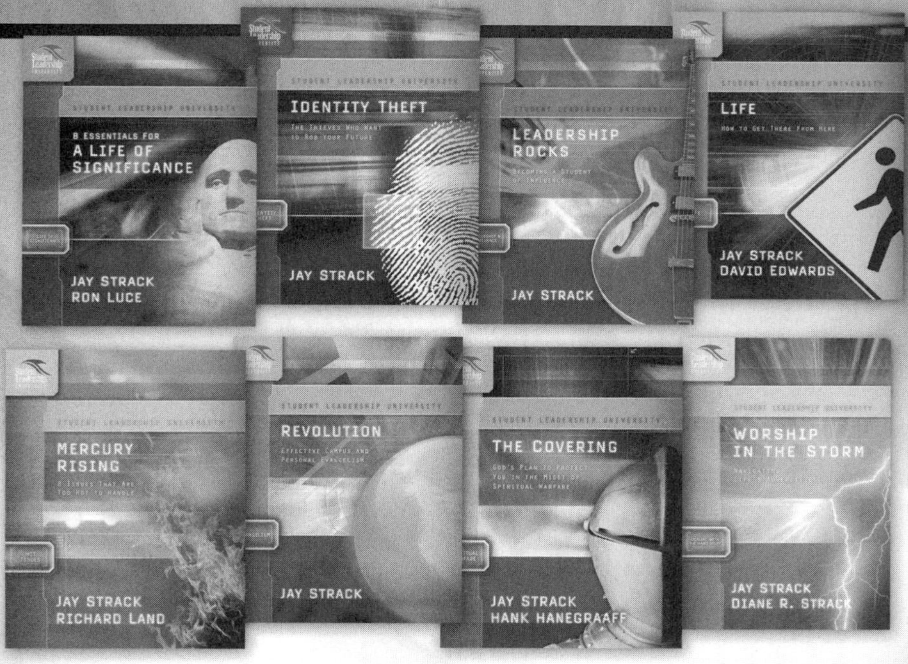